Dealing with Feeling...
Shy

Isabel Thomas

Illustrated by Clare Elsom

Heinemann
LIBRARY
Chicago, Illinois

© 2013 Heinemann Library
an imprint of Capstone Global Library, LLC
Chicago, Illinois

All rights reserved. No part of this publication may
be reproduced or transmitted in any form or by
any means, electronic or mechanical, including
photocopying, recording, taping, or any information
storage and retrieval system, without permission in
writing from the publisher.

Edited by Dan Nunn, Rebecca Rissman, and
  Catherine Veitch
Designed by Philippa Jenkins
Original illustrations © Clare Elsom
Illustrated by Clare Elsom
Production by Victoria Fitzgerald
Originated by Capstone Global Library, Ltd.
Printed in China

16 15 14 13 12
10 9 8 7 6 5 4 3 2 1

**Library of Congress Cataloging-in-Publication
Data**
Thomas, Isabel, 1980-
  Shy / Isabel Thomas.
       p. cm.—(Dealing with feeling)
  Includes bibliographical references and index.
  ISBN 978-1-4329-7109-0 (hb)—ISBN 978-1-4329-
7118-2 (pb) 1. Bashfulness in children—Juvenile
literature. 2. Bashfulness—Juvenile literature. I. Title.
  BF723.B3T56 2013
  155.2'32—dc23   2012008396

Every effort has been made to contact copyright
holders of material reproduced in this book. Any
omissions will be rectified in subsequent printings if
notice is given to the publisher.

All the Internet addresses (URLs) given in this book
were valid at the time of going to press. However,
due to the dynamic nature of the Internet, some
addresses may have changed, or sites may have
changed or ceased to exist since publication. While
the author and publisher regret any inconvenience
this may cause readers, no responsibility for any such
changes can be accepted by either the author or
the publisher.

Contents

Some words are shown in bold, **like this.** Find out what they mean in the glossary on page 23.

What Is Shyness?

jealous

angry

happy

proud

sad

Shyness is a **feeling.** It is normal to have many kinds of feelings every day.

4

Some feelings are not nice to have. Shyness is not a nice feeling. We might feel shy when we try new things or speak in front of people.

How Do We Know When Someone Is Feeling Shy?

Our faces and bodies can show other people how we are feeling. Some people may speak quietly when they are feeling shy.

Other people may not speak at all. Sometimes people might look unfriendly, when really they are just feeling shy.

What Does It Feel Like to Be Shy?

Shyness can make us feel a little scared around other people. We might worry about doing something **embarrassing**.

Shyness can mean we do not say
or do the things we would like to.
Being left out can make us feel
badly about ourselves.

Is It Normal to Feel Shy?

Sometimes we might feel shy for a short time. It is normal to feel shy when you do something for the first time.

Take time to get used to a new **activity**. Watch other people and see how they act. This will help you to feel more **confident**.

How Can I Deal with Shyness?

Many people feel shy when they meet new people for the first time. You might feel that you do not know what to say.

The best thing to do when you feel shy is to smile. A shy face may look scared or grumpy. A smiling face always looks friendly.

How Do I Start Talking to New People?

A big change, such as starting a new school, can be scary. You might feel shy because you do not know what the children and teachers will be like.

A good way to make new friends is to ask people questions about themselves. Maybe you like the same books or computer games!

How Can I Get Better at Talking in Front of People?

Many people feel **nervous** when they have to speak in front of lots of people. This might make you too shy to raise your hand in class.

Practice reading out loud to your family or friends. The more you practice speaking to a group, the easier it will get.

What If I Feel Shy All the Time?

Sometimes shy **feelings** can be very strong and stop us from doing things we enjoy. You might feel shy if how you look or the things you do make you different from other people.

The best way to deal with shy feelings
is to talk about them. Share your
worries with others. They might tell
you what they do to feel less shy.

How Can I Help Someone Who Is Feeling Shy?

Everyone feels shy sometimes. Ask your friends, teachers, or parents what makes them feel shy.

The next time you spot people who are not joining in, remember that they might be feeling shy. Help them to make friends by being friendly yourself.

Make a Shyness Toolbox

Write down some tips to help you deal with shy **feelings.**

Practice doing new things with your friends or family.

Relax and take deep breaths to keep your body calm.

Give yourself a treat every time you try something new.

Give someone a **compliment.** This is a good way to start talking to someone new.

Talk about your feelings with someone you trust.

Don't be afraid to ask for help. Everyone needs help sometimes.

Ask people questions about themselves.

Smile! A smiling face always looks friendly.

Glossary

activity something you do for fun

compliment something nice that you say about someone

confident feeling that you can do something well

embarrassing something that makes you feel awkward, as if you have done something wrong

feeling something that happens inside our minds. It can affect our bodies and the way we behave.

nervous scared or worried about doing something

Find Out More

Books

Medina, Sarah. *Shy (Feelings)*.
   Chicago: Heinemann Library, 2008.
Twohy, Mike. *Poindexter Makes a Friend*. New York:
   Simon & Schuster, 2011.

Internet sites

Facthound offers a safe, fun way to find Internet sites related to this book. All of the sites on Facthound have been researched by our staff.

Here's all you do:
Visit www.facthound.com
Type in this code: 9781432971090

Index